# WALK TOWTON 1461:

## A Visitor Guide to Battle-Related Sites

Helen Cox & Alan Stringer

Herstory Writing & Interpretation/
York Publishing Services

2012

Published by Helen Cox
Herstory Writing & Interpretation
www.helencox-herstorywriting.co.uk

Cover illustration: Towton Battlefield in winter by Roger Keech, ©
RK Productions 2011

First published in 2012 by Herstory Writing & Interpretation/
York Publishing Services
ISBN 978-0-9565768-2-8

Also by Helen Cox:

Non-fiction:
*The Battle of Wakefield Revisited: a fresh perspective on Richard of
York's final battle, December 1460*
*Walk Wakefield 1460: a Visitor Guide to Battle-Related Sites*

Fiction (under the pen-name Rae Andrew):
*The Lay of Angor, Book 1: Gondarlan,* revised 2nd edition

All titles printed by, and available from:

York Publishing Services,
64, Hallfield Road, Layerthorpe,
York YO31 7ZQ
Telephone: 01904 431213
Internet orders: www.YPD-books.com

# CONTENTS

# LIST OF ILLUSTRATIONS

**Line Drawings:**

**Photographs (all by, and copyright of, the authors as shown):**

# PREFACE

Five hundred and fifty years ago, England was gripped by the long-running, vicious fight for the crown between the rival royal Houses of Lancaster and York known today as the Wars of the Roses.

This booklet leads you through one of its bloodiest phases, with an illustrated guide to visiting sites connected with the Battle of Towton. With it, you can follow the whole of Edward, Earl of March's campaign of 1461 from his first battle at Mortimer's Cross to the decisive engagement at Towton on Palm Sunday.

Many places featured in this guide (Wigmore Castle, the battlefields at Mortimer's Cross, St Albans, Ferrybridge, Dintingdale and Towton, St Mary's Chapel, Dacre's tomb and Dacre's Cross) are accessible to pedestrians at any time. Otherwise, all opening times and admission charges quoted at the end of each section are correct at the date of publication, but may change in future; please check with the site concerned before your visit to avoid possible disappointment. NB: consultation is currently under way regarding extensions and improvements to the footpath network around Saxton; as a result, the walking route from The Crooked Billet to All Saints Church described in Part 4 may be subject to change.

**Helen Cox & Alan Stringer**
**January 2012**

# ACKNOWLEDGEMENTS

We thank Roger Keech of RK Productions for permission to use his photograph of Towton Battlefield on the cover of this publication. We are also grateful to Captain Andrew Powell of the King's Own Yorkshire Light Infantry for walking the Ferrybridge area with Alan Stringer, and making helpful suggestions. Finally we thank our patient spouses, Mick and Judith, for putting up with all the time we spent away on field-trips, in meetings or pounding the keyboard!

*Figure 1: Map of Britain showing sites featured in the text and locations of battles from 1459 – 1461: the stand-off at Ludford Bridge (12$^{th}$ October 1459); Battle of Northampton (10$^{th}$ July 1460); encounter at Worksop (21$^{st}$ December 1460); Battle of Wakefield (30$^{th}$ December 1460); Battle of Mortimer's Cross (3$^{rd}$ February 1461); 2$^{nd}$ Battle of St Albans (17$^{th}$ February 1461); Battles of Ferrybridge/Dintingdale (28$^{th}$ March 1461); and Battle of Towton (Palm Sunday, March 29$^{th}$ 1461).*

# INTRODUCTION

London, 1460: the rival royal Houses of Lancaster and York were about to enter a new phase of their long, violent contest for the crown known today as the Wars of the Roses. Richard, Duke of York, cousin of the ineffectual King Henry VI, had at last decided to press his own claim to the throne; and in July 1460, his supporters had defeated the royal army at the Battle of Northampton and taken King Henry into 'protective custody'. While the King's wife, Queen Margaret of Anjou, together with their young son Edward, the Lancastrian Prince of Wales, fled to Scotland for safety, Richard of York returned from his exile in Ireland; and in October, marched into Westminster Hall and laid his hand on the throne, confidently expecting to be acclaimed as the new king.

Unfortunately for the Duke, this did not happen - although his claim to the crown was strong enough to result in the Act of Accord, which bypassed Prince Edward and named York (or his sons) as heir-apparent. But this attempt at compromise reckoned without the proud and resolute Queen Margaret, who responded by mustering a large army of loyalists to free her husband from Yorkist control, overturn the Act of Accord and restore her son to the succession.

So in December 1460, Yorkist forces split to counter the various Lancastrian threats. The Duke's nephew Richard Neville, Earl of Warwick, remained in London safeguarding King Henry. His eldest son, the 18-year-old Edward, Earl of March, was dispatched to the Welsh Marches, (his first independent command); accompanied by nobles including Lords Audley, Fitzwalter and Grey, Edward's mission was to secure the region, prevent the King's stepfather, Owen Tudor, and half-brother Jasper Tudor, Earl of Pembroke, from joining Queen Margaret's army, then to reinforce his father in Yorkshire. The Duke himself, with his second son, the 17-year-old Edmund, Earl of Rutland, Warwick's father Richard Neville, Earl of Salisbury, and the Earl's sons Sir Thomas Neville and John, Lord Montague, meanwhile marched north to confront the main rebel army...

Shrewsbury, 1461: in early January, Edward of March received the dreadful news that on 30th December, both his father and the younger brother with whom he had been raised and educated had been killed at the Battle of Wakefield. Also dead was his uncle the Earl of Salisbury, captured after the battle and executed the following day at Pontefract Castle; his cousin Sir Thomas; and up to 2000 Yorkist supporters. Another staunch ally, Sir John Savile, Constable of the late Duke's castle at Sandal, (which overlooks the fields where the disastrous encounter took place), had been captured and imprisoned. Adding insult to injury, the Lancastrian victors had then paraded the severed heads of the Duke, Earls and other prominent Yorkist victims to York, where they were spiked up on Mickelgate Bar and the other city gates so that, as Shakespeare later put it, 'York might overlook York'.

This devastating event was to have far-reaching consequences, changing the course of English history and putting a new king on the throne. Its immediate effect was to ensure that the bloody vendetta would continue, and pass on to the next generation. Grief-stricken by the deaths of so many close relatives and friends and outraged by the dishonouring of their remains, Edward was determined to have vengeance. Indeed, he had little choice but to fight; by inheriting his late father's titles and position as heir-apparent, he had become the new target for Lancastrians bent on destroying the House of York's challenge to the throne once and for all.

And so the novice commander embarked on the campaign which would end in such carnage at Towton on March 29th. His first priority was to deal with the Earls of Pembroke and Wiltshire, who in late January landed an army of Bretons, Frenchmen and Irish supporters in Pembrokeshire, enabling them to threaten the Yorkist heartlands around Ludlow before marching on to reinforce Queen Margaret's army, probably via Lancastrian territories in the Midlands. Edward duly took his troops south to intercept them, and by the end of January is thought to have been installed at Wigmore Castle – close to the ground where battle would be joined on Tuesday, February 3rd, and where our campaign trail begins.

# PART 1: MORTIMER'S CROSS

## Wigmore Castle

Wigmore Castle was founded in 1067 by William fitz Osbern, Earl of Hereford, a close associate of William the Conqueror. It began as a typical Norman motte-and-bailey castle, situated on a narrow, steep ridge with a marsh, (now drained), to the north, and further defended by deep ditches and a timber palisade wall. The village of Wigmore, also founded in the 11th century, grew up around the crossroads below the castle, and by the 14th century had become a prosperous market town with 102 inhabitants, a weekly market and annual fair.

After Hereford's death, Wigmore passed to the prominent Mortimer family, (from whom Edward of March was descended via his paternal grandmother Anne Mortimer), in around 1075. The Mortimers rebuilt the castle in stone in the 12th and early 13th centuries, and towers and high-status lodgings were added in the early 14th century by Roger Mortimer, 1st Earl of March. Further works were also carried out in the 15th century (although by this time the town of Wigmore had declined in importance as the Mortimers shifted their administrative centre to their larger castle at Ludlow).

Nonetheless, Wigmore Castle remained one of the great Marcher fortresses, a link in the chain of strongholds that prevented Welsh incursions along England's border; lying between the rivers Teme and Lugg and therefore controlling access both to and along them, it functioned as an observation post overlooking routes into Wales, and as a springboard for military incursions. Had it been captured by the Welsh it would have opened the way into Herefordshire and the west Midlands, so English control was of paramount importance; if Edward had lost the Battle of Mortimer's Cross, it could have facilitated extensive raids into the Yorkist heartlands.

Thus Wigmore was a logical base for Edward and his troops in January 1461. The village was conveniently placed at the crossing of routes to Ludlow and Hereford, and surrounded by farmland to

9

provide victuals for sale at its market. The castle was, by this period, a substantial and well-defended fortress consisting of three main parts: an outer bailey containing service buildings such as stables, granaries and other stores; an inner bailey defended by a deep double ditch and two walls, containing the great hall and residential quarters; and set atop the motte, a high-security keep with a thick-walled great tower, protecting the lord's private lodgings. Further provisions for Edward's army could have been drawn from the deer-parks which bordered the castle to the north and west, along with the nearby fishponds, rabbit warren and dovecot.

However, perhaps most importantly, Wigmore lay only a few miles from Mortimer's Cross, the junction of roads connecting Wigmore and Ludlow (via Leominster) to Hereford, and thence through Ross-on-Wye, Gloucester and Cheltenham to the Fosse Way and central England (see Fig. 1). So by basing himself at Wigmore, Edward was well placed to respond quickly to the Lancastrian threat...

*Plate 1: The Keep at Wigmore Castle*

**Information for Visitors to Wigmore Castle:**

Wigmore Castle passed to the Crown in 1452, then in 1601 was purchased by Sir Thomas Harley. It finally fell into its current ruinous state following its slighting to prevent its use by Royalist forces in the Civil War of the 1640s. Wigmore is now maintained by English Heritage, open year-round and with no entrance fee.

All that remains of the site today are the impressive earthworks and a few fragments of the inner bailey curtain wall, gatehouse and lodging towers, a corner of the great hall, and on the motte, a wall of the private lodgings together with a small part of the keep tower. As Plate 1 shows, all the foundations and collapsed walls are heavily overgrown, the ruin having been deliberately left in a wild condition to act as a nature reserve for several rare animal species, including the lesser horsehoe bat, and wildflowers such as the ploughman's spikenard. As a result, Wigmore is extremely picturesque, with the motte affording spectacular views over the countryside towards Mortimer's Cross, as rewarding for naturalists and hikers as it is for historians.

There is no vehicular access or car-parking at the site, the designated parking area being at Wigmore Village Hall on the A4110 to Ludlow, a quarter of a mile from the crosroads where the footpath to the castle can be picked up. The walk from the parking area to the monument is c. 1 mile/1.6 km. The footpath, which passes St James's Church, is steep and irregular with several stile gates. The castle site has a footpath around it and is interpreted with information boards, but the ground surface is uneven with many flights of steps, and there are no toilets or other visitor facilities. Consequently a visit to Wigmore Castle is unsuitable for young children, pushchairs, wheelchair users and visitors with walking difficulties.

Further information on Wigmore Castle and its history can be found on www.english-heritage.org.uk/daysout/properties/wigmore-castle/visitor-information and www.castlewales.com/wigmore.html.

**Directions to Wigmore Castle:**

**From Ludlow:** Wigmore Castle is situated in Herefordshire, c. 8 miles/13 km south-west of Ludlow. Follow the A4113 Leintwardine road out of Ludlow, and turn left at the junction with the A4110 to Mortimer's Cross and Hereford to approach Wigmore from the north. The designated parking area at the Village Hall is on the left just outside the village; walk down to the crossroads and you will see the sign for the footpath to the castle ahead and slightly to the right on Mortimer Way.

**The Battle of Mortimer's Cross**

While the Yorkists were mustering around Wigmore, Lancastrian forces were also on the move. Their army contained many foreigners, since the Tudors, by virtue of Owen Tudor's marriage to Henry V's widow Catherine of Valois, could draw on support from connections in France and Brittany, while their ally James Butler, Earl of Wiltshire, was also the 5th Earl of Ormonde, and able to recruit from his extensive holdings in Ireland. However, the Tudors were also powerful in Wales, and on their arrival began gathering local support from the estates held by Jasper Tudor as Earl of Pembroke.

The Lancastrian presence would have struck terror into Welsh and Marcher Yorkists - especially around Ludlow, where memories of the sacking of the castle and town after Richard of York's strategic withdrawal from Ludford Bridge in 1459 still ran deep and bitter. Edward's forces were accordingly swelled by the Herbert brothers of Raglan, and veterans of the French wars like Henry ap Griffith, along with recruits from Shropshire and Herefordshire – local men who could be quickly mobilised and were largely self-supporting. He also had a loyal retainer in John Dwnn, based at Kidwelly, whose family seems to have tracked Lancastrian activities and kept Edward appraised of their movements.

Meanwhile the Tudors and the Earl of Wiltshire headed north-east for Llandovery, whence they could proceed via Brecon, Hereford and Worcester to the Lancastrian stronghold of Coventry in preparation to join the Queen's forces. Alternatively, they may have wished to garner additional troops in north Wales, where Pembroke's supporters still held the important fortress of Denbigh Castle. Since, unusually, the campaign was being fought in winter, the most direct route through mountainous central Wales may have been impassable; their less difficult and dangerous path was to continue east, then strike north along the Severn valley – which would take them through the Mortimer heartlands around Ludlow. Either way, they seem to have travelled from Brecon, down past Glasbury and along the Roman road past Weobley, into Leominster and up to Mortimer's Cross, a journey of 110 miles which they covered in a week; considering that a supply train is reckoned to make 12 miles per day, their average progress of 15 miles per day is impressive.

As the gateway to Yorkist holdings in the area and thence to the Midlands, Mortimer's Cross was Edward's choice of ground for the armies to engage. As well as protecting his local interests, he needed to prevent Tudor's forces from achieving their ultimate objective of reaching England to swell Queen Margaret's ranks; blocking their point of access to the main road network was therefore a logical decision. Equally, even though the Lancastrians may not have wished to fight a major battle at this point, they needed to dispose of the threat March presented so that they could proceed with their mission in safety; and thus, as they approached the junction from the south to laager at the village of Kingsland (near the present site of the rugby and cricket club), the stage was set for the Battle of Mortimer's Cross.

Unfortunately, contemporary and near-contemporary sources give very little information about the course of events. Reports on the size of the armies and the casualty figures vary widely, and may be wildly innacurate; even the precise location of the fighting that took place between Mortimer's Cross and Kingsland is disputed, while details of battlefield depositions and tactics are unknown. However, one incident that occurred on the eve of battle, Monday, February 2nd, is well attested. According to the *English Chronicle*, at around ten in the morning 'were seen three suns in the firmament shining clear.' This phenomenon (*parhelia*, or 'sun dogs') is understood

13

today as a product of light refracting through ice-crystals in cold air; but in 1461, appearing as it did on a holy day - the Feast of Purification of Our Blessed Lady – it was little short of miraculous. Edward presented it to his followers as betokening the Holy Trinity and being an omen for victory, and thereafter adopted the 'Sunne in Splendour' and the *rose en soleil*, a white Yorkist rose surrounded by sunbeams, as personal emblems. The appearance of the parhelia is surely the event Shakespeare later refers to in his Henry VI Part 3 (Act 2, Scene 1), although without specifically mentioning Mortimer's Cross:

*Three glorious suns, each one a perfect sun;*
*Not separated with the racking clouds,*
*But sever'd in a pale clear-shining sky.*
*See, see! they join, embrace and seem to kiss,*
*As if they vow'd some league inviolable:*
*Now are they but one lamp, one light, one sun.*
*In this the heaven figures some event.*

In order to block the Lancastrians' further advance, by Tuesday, February 3rd, the Yorkists had marched to Mortimer's Cross, crossed the River Lugg and drawn up in battle order. The ground here is a natural funnel, hemmed to the west by wooded hills and to the east by the river; Edward doubtless took advantage of the terrain to shorten his line, keeping the bridge to his back in case he needed to withdraw quickly, and obliging his opponents to attack across the open fields below (see Fig. 2 and Plate 5). (He may have originally formed his line further south in the direction of Kingsland, then withdrawn towards the neck of the funnel to draw the enemy on).

Possibly the day began with an attempt at parley. If so, it was a disastrous failure, leading to the treacherous killing of Edward's herald, Blue Mantle (a local tradition reflected by the name of Blue Mantle Cottage, situated to the north of the battlefield beside the Roman road to Hereford). Either way, the Lancastrians now had no choice but to attack; if they withdrew they would almost certainly lose men through scattering, desertion and Yorkist cavalry pursuit, be forced to make a wide detour to avoid Wigmore Castle, and then

14

try to continue their journey with an intact enemy at their rear.

The only tenuous clue to battlefield deployments at Mortimer's Cross comes from an Elizabethan poem by Michael Drayton, which places the Earl of Wiltshire with his Irish contingent in the van, or right-hand, 'battle' (battalion) of the typical 15$^{th}$ century deployment, leaving the Earl of Pembroke and his father Owen Tudor to command the main (centre) and rearward (left) battles. Facing them would have been Edward of March, who may have led the centre, possibly with Lords Audley and Fitzwalter, (both of whom owned manors in Herefordshire), or Lord Grey of Wilton near Ross-on-Wye, commanding the rearward and van.  If battle proper then commenced with the characteristic archery exchange, the Yorkists could have gained an early advantage. They probably had more archers than the polyglot Lancastrian army, the longbow being a popular traditional weapon in Wales and the Marches; they may also have exploited the terrain by positioning archers on the high ground to the west of the battlefield, to pour arrows into the advancing enemy rearward.

As the fighting progressed, some action – possibly a last stand – took place around the road junction at the north end of Kingsland, (Plate 2 shows the pedestal monument erected there in 1799), as indicated by finds of bridle-bits, stirrups, buckles and iron fragments, possibly sword blades, unearthed in the 1850s. However, in the absence of further archaeological evidence, all we can be sure of is the outcome: that Edward's highly-motivated, largely local army with its many experienced commanders won a resounding victory over the Lancastrians' assortment of French, Breton, Irish and Welsh troops, some of whom may have been relatively poorly-armed. Contemporary chroniclers noted that the Earls of Pembroke and Wiltshire were 'put to flight' and 3000 to 4000 of their men slain (although these casualty figures may be grossly inflated); it is believed that many of the dead lie buried in a field just south of Mortimer's Cross, known as The Clamp. Their third captain, Owen Tudor, was captured and later beheaded in the market-place at Hereford where, according to *Gregory's Chronicle*, 'his head was set on the highest pinnacle of the market cross'; arguably, this treatment of Henry VI's stepfather was Edward's act of revenge for the display of his own father's and brother's heads on Mickelgate Bar after the Battle of Wakefield.

**Information for Visitors to Mortimer's Cross:**

Mortimer's Cross battlefield is roughly triangular, defined by the A4110 between Wigmore and Hereford, the Roman road Hereford Lane, and the junction with the B4862 at Mortimer's Cross. There is no formal battlefield trail, although much of the ground can be walked using footpaths through fields and along stretches of minor roads. The safest route is to park in Kingsland and begin at the monument on the north-western edge of the village (the conjectured location of the Lancastrian camp and closing stages of the battle):

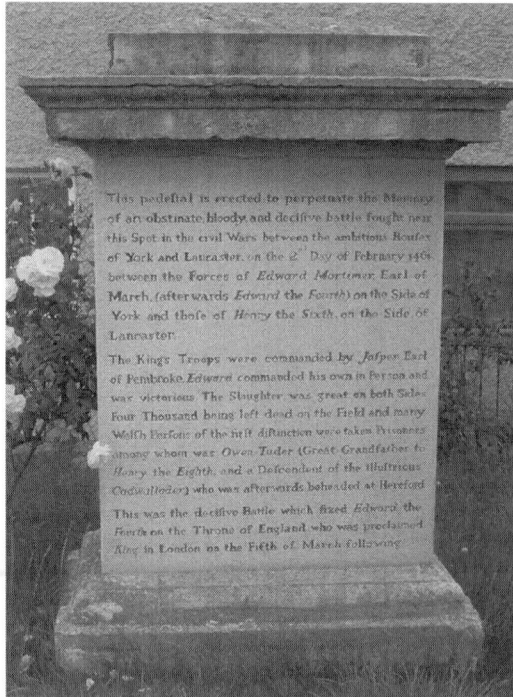

*Plate 2: The battle monument at Kingsland*

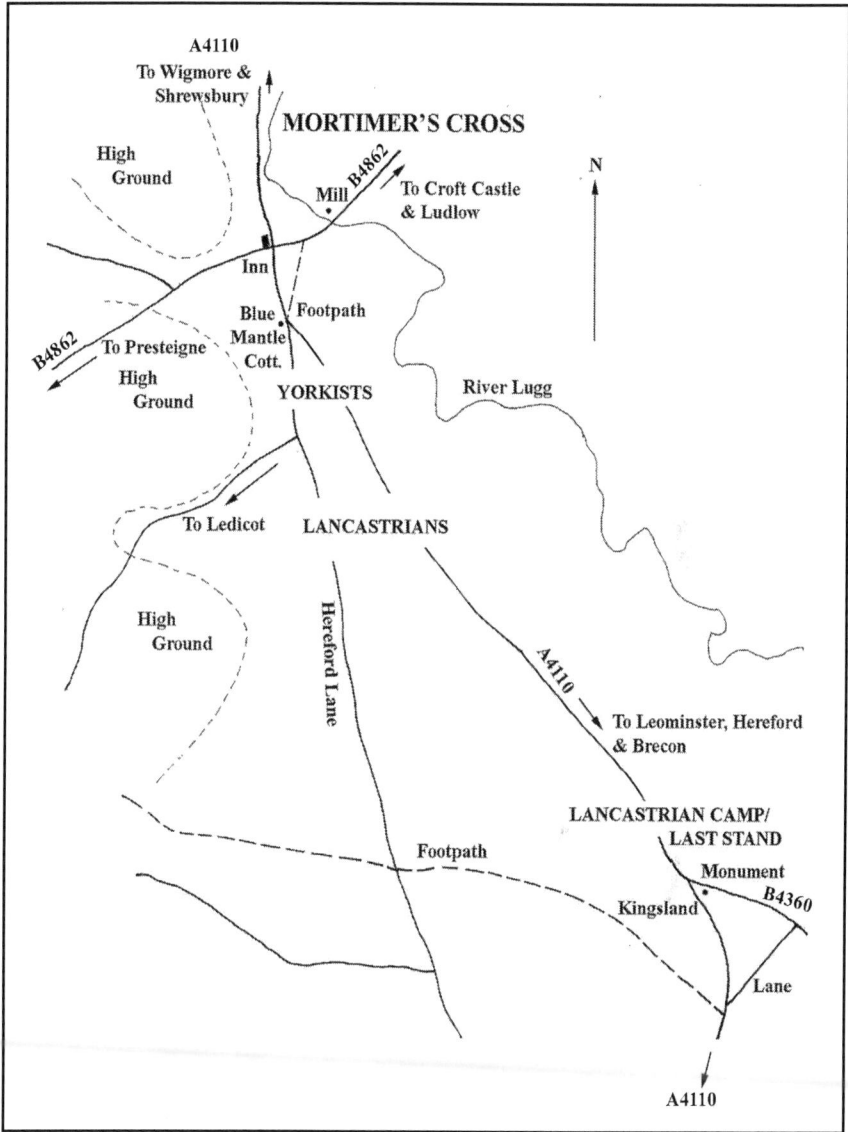

*Figure 2: Battlefield walking route from Kingsland (Lancastrian position) to Mortimer's Cross (Yorkist position), following footpaths and Hereford Lane.*

Facing the monument, take the left fork (B4360) into Kingsland, then first right onto a small lane. At the end, cross the A4110 and the stile opposite, follow the footpath for c. half a mile, then turn right onto Hereford Lane. Half a mile north up Hereford Lane, a lane on the left goes to Ledicot. This is believed to mark the area of the main melee, with the Yorkists ahead to the north and the Lancastrians to the south; rising ground to the north-west (see Fig. 2 and Plate 5) would have protected Edward's right flank, and is the conjectured position of a squad of Yorkist archers.

Continue north up Hereford Lane to the junction with the A4110, with Blue Mantle Cottage and the site of the so-called Battle Oak (now lost) on the left. On the right, a footpath across the fields leads to the B4862; turn right towards Ludlow for the bridge over the River Lugg and, just beyond on the left, Mortimer's Cross Mill:

*Plate 3: Mortimer's Cross Mill*

Although there has probably been a mill on this site since the 15<sup>th</sup> century, the present working water mill dates to 1750 and contains a small display of battlefield maps and information.

After visiting the Mill, go back along the B4862 to the crossroads with the A4110, where you will find the Mortimer's Cross Inn. From this point you can walk back down the A4110 to Blue Mantle then retrace your steps south down Hereford Lane to Kingsland (the more direct route down the A4110 is unsafe for pedestrians owing to the volume of traffic and absence of wide verges). This walk is c. 5 miles/8 km in total, and is unsuitable for young children, pushchairs, wheelchair users and visitors with walking difficulties.

Alternatively, reverse the directions above and begin at the Mill, where there is a large car-park. The Mill environs are very attractive, although the paths can be slippery, the river banks are steep and the water fast-flowing, so children must be carefully supervised; and as the site forms part of a working farm, dogs are not allowed.

Mortimer's Cross Mill is an English Heritage property open to the public on Sundays between April and September from 10 am – 4 pm. Admission charges are £4.00 for adults, £3.50 for concessions and £2.50 for under-15's. Disabled access is limited to the exterior and ground floor, and the path from the car-park is very uneven; disabled visitors can be set down nearer the mill and enter via a private gate to Mill House – please telephone in advance to arrange.

For further information about Mortimer's Cross Mill, or to arrange access for disabled visitors, telephone 01568 708820, email chrislemiller@googlemail.com, or see www.mortimerscrossmill.com and www.english-heritage.org.uk/daysout/properties/mortimers-cross -water-mill.

Further information on the Battle of Mortimer's Cross can be found on www.battlefieldstrust.com/resource-centre/warsoftheroses.

**Directions to Mortimer's Cross:**

**From Wigmore:** Follow the A4110 south to Kingsland. At the junction where the monument is sited, bear left on the B4360 into the village to find car-parking.

**Other Local Sites of Interest:**

**Ludlow Castle, Castle Square, Ludlow, Shropshire SY8 1AY**

The great Mortimer stronghold of Ludlow Castle dominates the north-western skyline of this thriving market town, where many other fine medieval buildings also survive. Ludlow has strong Wars of the Roses connections as part of the estates owned by Richard, Duke of York: it was the place ransacked by the forces of Henry VI in 1459, where Edward of March's mother Cecily, Duchess of York, and his younger brothers George and Richard, (later King Richard III), were taken into captivity, and where the townspeople welcomed Duke Richard back in 1460 prior to his claim for the throne.

*Plate 4: Ludlow Castle*

The remains of the curtain wall, north range, chapel and great tower are extensive; there are also full visitor facilities including a tea room and gift shop, and a programme of regular events such as the annual Medieval Christmas Fayre.

Ludlow Castle is open 7 days a week for much of the year, from 10am - 4pm in autumn/winter, 10am - 5pm in spring/summer, and 10am – 7pm in August. December to January openings are weekends only, 10am – 4pm, except between 26th December to 1st January, when it is open daily between these hours. There may be other periods of closure throughout the year, so it is advisable to check using the contact details below before making your visit.

Admission charges are £5.00 for adults, £4.50 for concessions, £13.50 for a family (two adults and two children), £2.50 for children over six years, and free for children under six; prices may vary for special events.

For further information on Ludlow Castle, Gift Shop, or to book a school or other group visit, telephone 01584 873355, email info@ludlowcastle.com, or see the website www.ludlowcastle.com.

**Croft Castle, Yarpole, Herefordshire HR6 9PW**

Croft Castle, situated between the A4110 and B4362 north-east of Mortimer's Cross, was the home of Sir Richard Croft, a Yorkist ally at the Battle of Mortimer's Cross. The medieval castle was converted into a mansion in the 17th century and later remodelled in the Gothic style; it is now maintained by the National Trust, with full visitor facilities including a tea room, shop and children's play area, and contains a collection of rare furniture from the 17th to 19th centuries.

Croft Castle is open 7 days a week between February and November, from 1pm – 4.30 pm. From mid-November to mid-December it is open weekends only, except for a week before Christmas when it opens daily from 1pm – 4.30pm; the site then closes for Christmas and throughout January. At other times the parkland and woods may close in high wind, and the whole site may close in snow.

Admission to the building and grounds costs £7.20 for adults, £18.00 for a family group, and £3.60 for children, with lower charges for admission to the garden and grounds only in summer, and grounds only in winter.

For further information on Croft Castle, telephone 01568 780246, email croftcastle@nationaltrust.org.uk or look up Croft Castle on the National Trust website www.nationaltrust.org.uk.

*Plate 5: The battlefield at Mortimer's Cross, looking north towards the Yorkist position*

# PART 2: ST ALBANS

After his victory at Mortimer's Cross, Edward's objective was to reach London where his ally, Richard Neville, Earl of Warwick, was 'caretaking' Henry VI. As the new would-be king led his troops from Herefordshire to combine with Warwick's forces, Queen Margaret and her army were also on the move – and also bound for London, intent on regaining control of the city, rescuing King Henry from the Yorkists, and completing the job of destroying the House of York's claim which they had begun so successfully at Wakefield.

And so, as the unpaid Lancastrian army pillaged its way down from Yorkshire, Warwick rode north to bar the road to the capital – taking Henry VI with him for safekeeping – and the point where their forces were destined to clash was St Albans...

**The Second Battle of St Albans**

St Albans, an historic market town, lies 22 miles/35 km north of London. The city has a long history of settlement, being named Verlamion or Verulam by the Catuvellauni tribe; after the Roman conquest it became the first major town on the Roman Watling Street for north-bound travellers and known as Verulamium. St Alban, from whom the town took its modern name, was martyred for his Christian faith in around AD 308; his shrine can be seen in the spectacular cathedral.

The medieval town grew up on high ground to the north east of the Abbey, a centre of religious and political authority where the first draft of the Magna Carta was written. The Abbey remained in use and was bought by the townspeople in 1539 after the dissolution under Henry VIII; it became a cathedral in 1877 when the City Charter was granted, and is now known as the Cathedral and Abbey Church of St Albans.

Today the core of the city around the Abbey and Market Place is of medieval origin, and many of its 15th century buildings can still be seen. During the Wars of the Roses two battles took place in or close to St Albans, the first being on May 22$^{nd}$ 1455 within the town; the second, on February 17$^{th}$ 1461, started at the Market Place and straggled north up to Nomansland Common via Bernard's Heath.

The Lancastrian army was then led, as it had been at Wakefield, by relatively young nobles such as the Duke of Somerset, the Earl of Northumberland and John, Lord Clifford, all of whose fathers had been killed at the First Battle of St Albans. Their army comprised men from the West Country, Scotland and the Borders; and it was the behaviour of these men, plundering a 30-mile-wide swathe of country as they marched south, that terrified Londoners and had a significant impact on the subsequent course of events.

Meanwhile, Warwick's forces moved to hold St Albans and its northern approaches to block the Lancastrians' southward passage. Taking up positions to interdict the main north-south road, (the old Roman Watling Street), he set up defensive lines of cannons, caltrops and pavises, (large wooden shields behind which archers could shelter from opposing archers), which in part took advantage of the ancient earthwork known as Beech Bottom Dyke. His mobile forces were formed into the traditional three battles or divisions, Warwick leading the mainward or centre battle, the Duke of Norfolk the van or forward battle on his right, and his brother John the rearward battle on the left. A force of archers was left in St Albans as a rearguard and to secure the town against any possible enemy incursions.

As Warwick manoeuvred, Lancastrian scouts monitored the situation. From their information, and that of Sir Henry Lovelace, a turncoat, it was realised that Yorkist lines were strong only facing to the north. Under Andrew Trollope, (possibly the architect of the Lancastrian victory at Wakefield), the Lancastrian army swung west late on February 16$^{th}$ and, in a night move undetected by Yorkist scouts, captured Dunstable. From here the Lancastrians advanced south-east towards St Albans, attacking the western outskirts of the town shortly after dawn, the classic time of day to spring an attack, when the defenders were either still asleep or having breakfast.

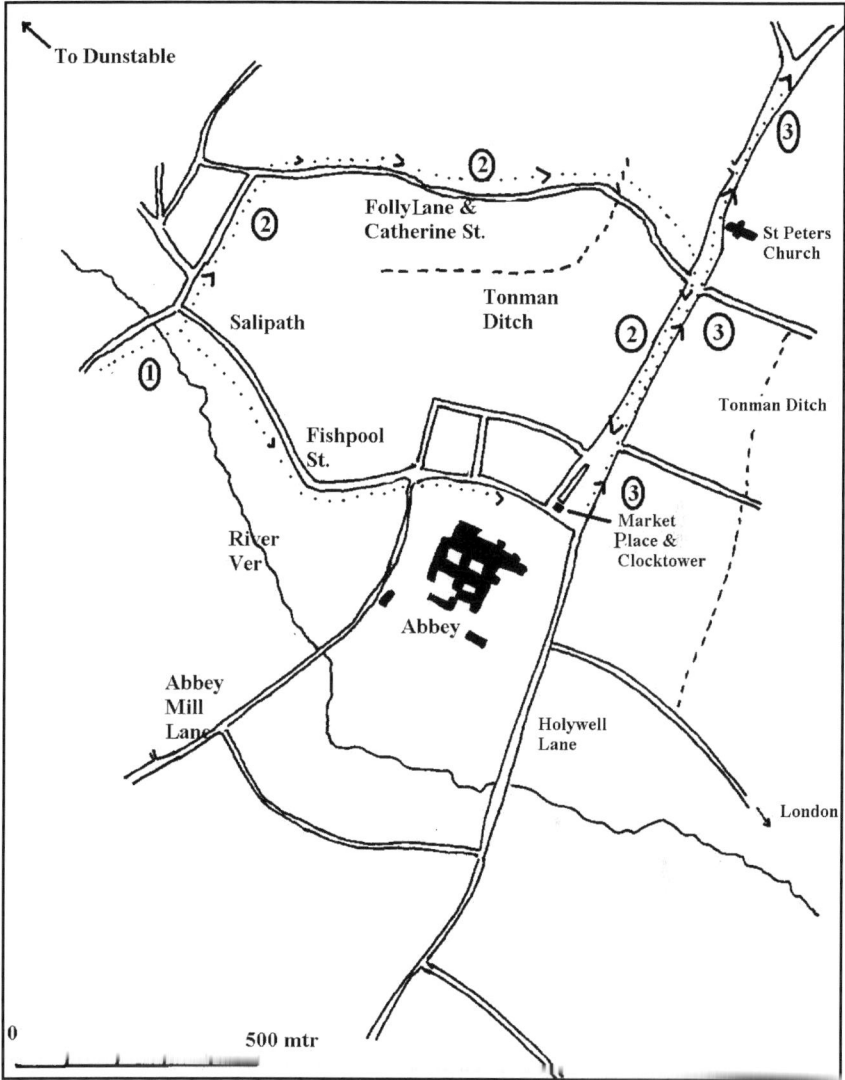

*Figure 3: Medieval St Albans, three phases of battle: 1 – the Lancastrians cross the River Ver, advance up Fishpool Street and are repulsed by Yorkist defenders; 2 – Trollope leads a flanking attack via Folly Lane; 3 – Yorkist withdrawal to Nomansland Common via Sandridge and Bernard's Heath.*

25

## The First Phase of Fighting

Trollope's troops crossed the River Ver via the footbridge and ford near St Michael's Church, headed up the Salipath (now Fishpool Street), Romeland (Roomland) and Church Street (now George Street), and reached the south end of the Market Place, close to the site of the old Eleanor Cross, by the medieval Clock Tower. Here they ran into a hail of Yorkist arrows from archers in buildings around the market square and were forced to fall back to escape this arrowstorm.

*Plate 6: Bridge and ford over the Ver; the start line for the Lancastrian attack*

Having been repulsed, Trollope decided on a two-pronged attack. The first move was to advance again up Fishpool Street to tie down the defenders around the Market Place; and while they were so occupied, to send scouts round the north-west edge of town to look for an undefended entrance. Following Folly Lane, Catherine Street, and the outside of the Tonman ditch, the scouts led troops to a lightly defended point on St Peter's Street (opposite St Peter's Church). This

26

flanking move split Yorkist forces between two lines of attack, forced Warwick to fight the battle on Lancastrian terms, and led to fierce house-to-house fighting in the centre of town. Yorkist positions were captured in turn and by midday Lancastrian troops were in control of centre of town, forcing Warwick to send troops south from Bernards Heath and Sandridge to counter moves by Somerset and Trollope in and around St Albans.

*Plate 7 : The medieval Clock Tower*

**The Second Phase of Fighting**

As the final pockets of Yorkist resistance were mopped up, Lancastrian troops were deployed to head north in order to engage Yorkist troops outside the town. To counter this, the Yorkist rearguard commanded by Warwick's brother John Neville, Lord Montague, moved to meet Somerset and Trollope's troops, and engaged in heavy hand-to-hand fighting on Bernard's Heath. It began to snow, the wet conditions rendering the Yorkists' cannon and handguns useless as their powder was dampened. Warwick found it difficult to extricate his other units from their fortifications and turn them about to face the Lancastrians, so that the Yorkist battles straggled into action one by one instead of in coordinated fashion. The rear battle, attempting to reinforce the defenders of the town, was engaged and dispersed. Lovelace's Kentish troops defected at this point, causing further confusion in the Yorkist ranks; with Lancastrian reinforcements from Dunstable pushing Montague's troops back they too broke and fled, leaving Montague and Lord Berners isolated and subsequently captured.

By late afternoon, the Lancastrians were attacking north-east out of St Albans to engage the Yorkist main and vanguard battles under Warwick and Norfolk. As dusk set in, (which would have been early, given the time of year and in the poor weather), Warwick realised that his men were outnumbered and increasingly demoralised, and withdrew north via Sandridge and Nomansland Common to Chipping Norton in Oxfordshire.

*Plate 8: Nomansland Common, where the last of the fighting took place.*

28

**The Third Phase and Aftermath**

In their haste to save what they could from the disaster, the Yorkists left behind a bemused King Henry, who is alleged to have spent the battle sitting under a tree, singing. The Yorkists Lord Bonville and Sir Thomas Kyriell had remained with him in order to protect him, receiving assurances that they would come to no harm. The next morning, however, Margaret asked her seven-year-old son, Edward, to decide their fate; he sentenced them to be beheaded. John Neville had also been captured but was spared execution by the Duke of Somerset, seeking to spare the same fate to his younger brother who had been captured by the Yorkists.

The young Prince Edward was knighted by his father, and then proceeded to knight 30 Lancastrian leaders. One of those so honoured was Andrew Trollope, an experienced captain who since transferring his allegiance to Henry in 1459 at the Battle of Ludford Bridge had masterminded the Lancastrian victories of Wakefield and St Albans.

*Plate 9: Bernard's Heath, where Henry VI was liberated*

The road to London was now open to Margaret and Henry. They could have marched south unopposed but, given the news from Mortimer's Cross and the refusal of Londoners to open the gates of the capital due to the Lancastrians' reputation for pillaging, they decided instead to withdraw north to their heartlands. They went via Dunstable, in the process losing large numbers of troops from Scotland and the Borders who deserted home with their plunder.

In the meantime the Earl of March had reached the Cotswolds, where he met up with the Earl of Warwick and such of his troops who had survived the calamity of St Albans. Together they marched to London where Edward, having learnt from his father's mistakes, gauged public opinion on his claim to the throne: on 1st March 1461, Warwick's brother George, Bishop of Exeter, persuasively addressed a large crowd at St George's Fields, with the result that they called for the Earl to be made king. On 2nd March his title was formally proclaimed throughout the city; on the 3rd it was ratified by a Great Council; and on 4th March, he proceeded to Westminster Palace to swear the oath and take possession of the realm as Edward IV. So England now had two kings but only one crown – and if Edward wished to wear it, he would have to take it from Henry VI by force...

**Information for Visitors to St Albans:**

Walking the town section of St Albans battlefield is easy, since the routes taken by the Lancastrian forces still exist and, apart from a moderate rise from the Kingsbury Watermill up Fishpool Street to the Clock Tower and Market Place, the ground is relatively flat. The full distance involved to trace the course of the action from St Albans north to Nomansland Common is c. 4 miles/6.4 km.

**Stage 1: St Michaels Bridge and ford, Fishpool Street, Clock Tower and Market Place (c. 900 yards/0.8 km uphill)**

St. Michael's Bridge over the Ver, built in 1765, is the oldest bridge in Hertfordshire. An earlier bridge, mentioned in a 1461 account of the Second Battle, was recorded in 1505 as *Pons de la Maltemyll.*

This – the start-line for the Lancastrian assault – is a useful place to begin your battlefield tour. Cross the river by either the bridge or the ford, (if you have your wellies on!), then walk up the hill along Fishpool Street noting the variety of building periods as you go. The lower end of Fishpool Street, (so named since Saxon times after the great fishpool from which the inhabitants of the royal estate of Kingsbury gained a livelihood), began life as a Roman road, and was recorded as 'Salipath or street of Kingsbury' in 1290.

A walk of c. 700 yards/0.63 km up the hill – level with what is now the Abbey School - brings you to within bowshot from the Yorkist troops defending this approach; archers were probably positioned in the upper levels of the buildings with infantry in the ground levels, a kind of 'defence in depth'. As such the Lancastrians would be walking into a neatly contrived trap; a disciplined volley of arrows from hidden archers would come as a nasty surprise and cause casualties, leaving the attackers no choice but to withdraw to cover and reassess their options, while any trying to occupy defended houses would meet with a hot reception.

**Stage 2: Market Place, Medieval Clock Tower and St Peter's Street**

The medieval Market Place was originally a large triangular open space; despite being rather smaller now, the present market space follows pretty much the boundaries of the original, and the market days on Wednesdays and Saturdays, (established in 1287), make this part of St Albans well worth a visit in its own right. The Domesday Book of 1086 valued the market tolls and other payments at £11, 14-0 per year. By the later Middle Ages temporary stalls were replaced by permanent structures to give the pattern of streets visible today.

The Clock Tower was built between 1403 – 1412 by Thomas Wolvey and is the only medieval example in the country, containing a rare mechanical clock. Its five floors are linked by two staircases; one, entered from the street, rises to the full height of the building; the other originates in the ground floor room and joins it at second floor level. This allowed the curfew bell to be rung and the clock maintained separately from the lower rooms, which served as a shop. The original bell was cast for the tower at Aldgate in London between 1371 and 1418, and its Latin inscription reads, *'I have the name of Gabriel, sent from heaven'*. From the top of the Clock Tower, the approach route employed by the Lancastrian troops can be clearly seen; Yorkist troops probably used this as a lookout and command post in the early stages of the battle.

The Clock Tower's later history includes use by the Admiralty as a semaphore station during the Napoleonic war of 1808-1814, as it could help relay a message to or from Yarmouth in five minutes. By the 1860s its fabric was in a fragile state and narrowly escaped demolition before being restored by Sir Gilbert Scott in 1864. In 2004 the roof was rebuilt with improved public safety and access, and affords a superb panoramic view of the town and Abbey.

The Clock Tower is open to the public on Saturdays, Sundays and Bank Holidays between Easter and mid-September, from 10.30 am – 5pm. Admission charges are 80p for adults, 40p for children. There are 93 narrow steps to climb, so the upper floors are not accessible for wheelchair users and visitors with mobility problems. To book group visits, telephone Brian Marpole on 01727 751815 between 9.30 am – 4.30 pm on Tuesdays to Fridays during school term-time.

For further information on the Clock Tower and other St Albans museums, including the Roman museum, see the website www.stalbansmuseums.org.uk.

The apex of the Market Place extends into St Peter's Street, described in 1245 as the 'great street', (*magno vico*), at the head of which is the Church of St Peter. The original church was founded around 948 AD by Abbot Ursinus, and forms one of three churches founded to receive pilgrims visiting the shrine of St Albans at the Abbey. The original Anglo-Saxon structure, of which nothing now remains, would have been made of wood. Over the next thousand years it underwent various changes in its fabric and style until it reached the form which can be seen today. It was around this area that the Lancastrian attackers and the Yorkist defenders clashed in a sprawling house-to-house fight, and the retreating Yorkist troops would have passed by St Peter's on their way to Bernard's Heath and Nomansland Common.

St Peter's is open year-round during office hours for visitors to the Church and its library, and parking is available in the churchyard (enter via the slip road by The Blacksmith's Arms public house). However, if you are planning a visit it is advisable to check whether services or special events might restrict your access by telephoning 01727 855485, or emailing mail@stpeterschurch.uk.com.

For further information on St Peter's Church, see the website www.stpeterschurch.uk.com.

**Stage 3: Catherine Street, Bernard's Heath, Nomansland Common**

The route used by the Lancastrians to take the Yorkist defenders in the rear (Catherine Street) can be followed round to the northern end of St Peter's Street. At the roundabout, turn right for the Market Place, or left to trace the route of the Yorkist retreat northward. Follow the A1081 past St Peter's Church, and after c. quarter of a mile/0.4 km, take the B651 on the right. On the left you will soon see the open park area of Bernard's Heath where King Henry was liberated; then continue along the B651 through Sandridge and onto the open countryside of Nomansland Common, where the final fighting and dispersal of the Yorkist forces took place.

To explore the whole St Albans battlefield area, OS Explorer Map 182 is recommended; excellent town maps are also available from the Tourist Information Centre in the Town Hall, situated in the Market Place (telephone 01727 864311, email tic@stalbans.gov.uk).

**Directions to St Albans:**

St Albans is situated close to the M1 (Junctions 6 – 10), A1(M), (Junctions 3 and 4), and M25 (Junctions 21a and 22). The city is also easily accessible by rail and bus from London and its environs.

**Other Local Sites of Interest:**

**Cathedral and Abbey Church of St Alban, St Albans, Hertfordshire AL1 1BY**

The Cathedral merits a visit for its scale, architecture, and stunning decoration. At 276 feet/84 m in length, the nave is the longest of any cathedral in England, and much of its fabric dates from Norman times. It became a cathedral in 1877 and is the second longest cathedral in the UK after Winchester Cathedral. The walls bear original church art, and the shrine of St Alban (Britain's first Christian martyr) can be seen.

Apart from the steps from the entrance to the nave, access is excellent. Wheelchair users can enter through the West Doors or the Slype (between the Chapter House and the South Transept); there are ramps through most of the building, lift access to the Shrine Chapel and disabled toilet facilities.

Admission is free but donations are welcome; and although the Cathedral is open year-round, access to certain areas may be restricted while services or special events are in progress. It is therefore advisable to check before you visit by telephoning 01727 860780, emailing mail@stalbanscathedral.org, or by consulting the Cathedral website www.stalbanscathedral.org.

# PART 3: FERRYBRIDGE & DINTINGDALE

The time had come for Edward IV to consolidate his claim to the crown – and, just as in his late father's Wakefield campaign, the fighting would take place in Yorkshire (see Fig. 4). In the weeks following his proclamation, various Yorkist nobles left London with their retinues to gather troops, equipment and provisions from their estates: Warwick to the Midlands, (subsequently joining Edward at the Trent, sometime around 18$^{th}$ March), Robert Horne and John Fogge to Kent, and John Mowbray, Duke of Norfolk, to Norfolk and East Anglia. Norfolk was slowed by ill health, so his rearguard headed north later than the rest of the army; his timely arrival at Towton on 29$^{th}$ March would however prove to be decisive.

Meanwhile the Yorkist vanguard under Lord Fauconberg set out from London on 11$^{th}$ March. Edward followed on the 13$^{th}$, and the two elements – van and mainward – proceeded along the Great North Road gathering additional troops, via St Albans, (reached on the 16$^{th}$), Cambridge, (reached on the 17$^{th}$), Nottingham, (reached on the 22$^{nd}$), and Pontefract, (reached on the 27$^{th}$), where they set up camp at Bubwith Heath, a triangular piece of land on what is now the Knottingley road.

Having reached Pontefract the Yorkist high command swung into action, sending light cavalry to reconnoitre the areas north of Ferrybridge, probably via Castleford; one of these parties may have encountered a Lancastrian scouting party from the Earl of Northumberland's force and destroyed it, thereby securing the ford at Castleford for Edward's use. Edward doubtless received intelligence from locals and travellers, but needed more accurate information in order to make his plans, guided by experienced commanders such as Lord Fauconberg, a veteran of the Hundred Years War against France. The Yorkist scouts would be under orders to reconnoitre the land, spot obstacles, and report back any intelligence gleaned about the Lancastrian army – but to avoid any contact with enemy forces unless absolutely necessary. The role of a party based at Dintingdale would prove be of major importance, as we will see later.

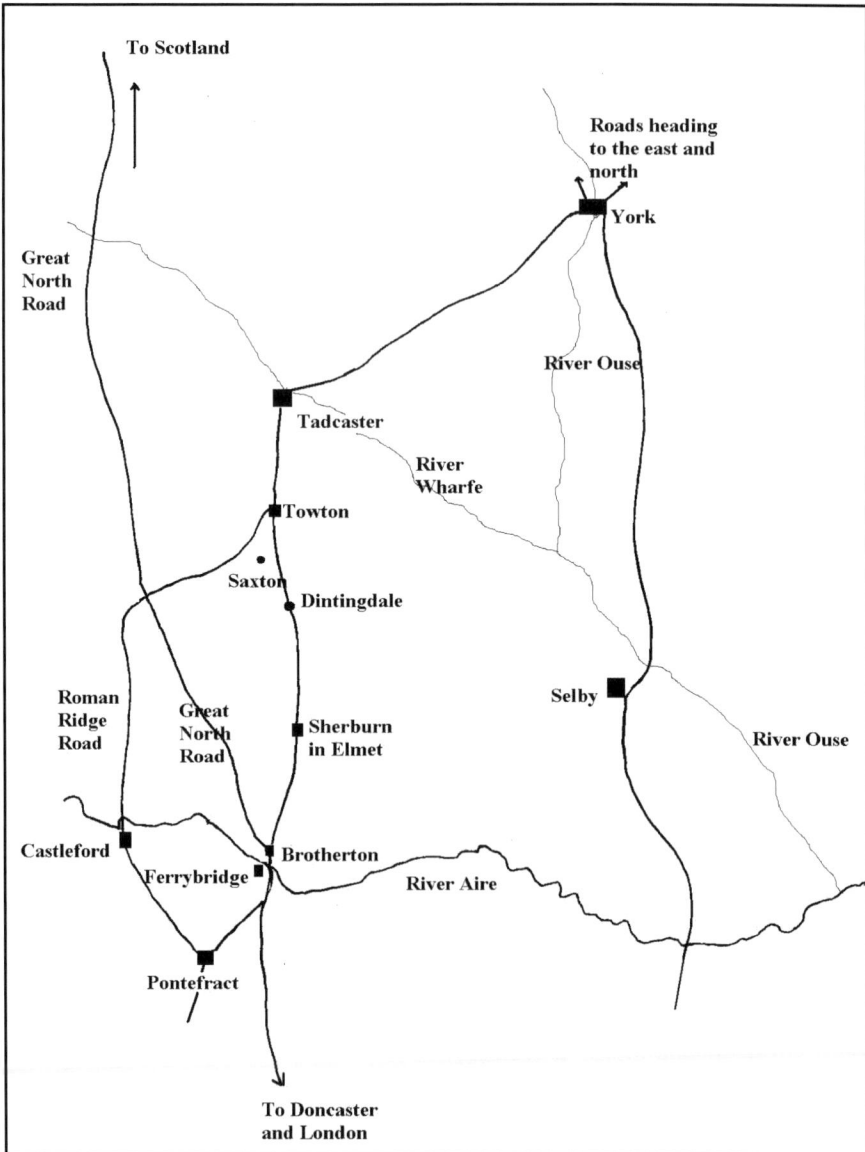

*Figure 4: Yorkshire – scene of conflict, March 1461*

On 27th March, Edward sent the Earl of Warwick and John Radcliffe, Lord Fitzwalter, with a mixed force of engineers and light cavalry, to secure and repair the bridge over the River Aire at Ferrybridge, (slighted by the Lancastrians to delay the Yorkists), in order to safeguard the crossing for his main advance. The small town of Ferrybridge is situated at a major crossing point where the Great North Road crosses over the River Aire, forming in medieval times a communications hub for road (north-south) and river (west-east) traffic. With its bridge of stone, built in the late 1300s to replace an earlier wooden structure built in 1198, and its stone-built causeway up to Brotherton, it was the only crossing for miles not subject to flood disruption (the next nearest crossing at Castleford, to the west, had a ford, but this had declined in importance since its heyday in Roman times).

*Plate 10: Old and new crossings at Ferrybridge. The 1797 bridge can be seen through the steel span of the 20th century construction, with the power station in the background. The medieval bridge probably followed the line of the modern steel bridge.*

37

This made Ferrybridge a popular stopping-off point for travellers, merchants and those engaged on government business heading both north and south, being well provided with facilities – inns, stables and the like - for travellers to break their journey. As a major communications intersection it was commercially, militarily, and politically important; instrumental in the movement of goods to and from local markets, linking Pontefract Castle, (in those days a major royal castle), with more northerly garrisons for reinforcement and resupply in the event of Scottish incursions over the border, and providing swift links for communications heading to all points of the compass. Just across the River Aire to the north lies Brotherton; and it was here that the roads heading north split into the Great North Road, (heading northwest), and the road to York via Sherburn-in-Elmet, Towton and Tadcaster (see Fig. 4).

Meanwhile, the Lancastrian high command had also been busy. By this time mustered at York, they too had doubtless been gathering information and may have tracked the Yorkist advance from the south. Like Edward though, the Duke of Somerset needed up-to-date and accurate intelligence on the Yorkist army, its composition and numbers, rate of advance, and the route it was taking. The two main routes that Edward could use with minimal deviation from his line of advance were the road – the present A162 - via Ferrybridge to Tadcaster, (the most direct and least at risk from floods thanks to its stone bridge at Ferrybridge and stone causeway over the floodplains on the north bank of the Aire), and the ford to the old Roman road heading north from Castleford (at risk from heavy waters when the Aire was in spate).

Fresh from his vengeful triumph at Wakefield in December 1460, John Clifford, 9th Lord of Skipton, and his 'Flower of Craven' were the ideal choice to act as Somerset's eyes and ears. Trained and equipped as light cavalry and experienced in policing the notoriously unstable Anglo-Scottish border, they were light, fast and versatile troops who were expected to act on their own initiative. Lightly equipped, however, they could only able to engage the enemy if at an advantage…

## The Battle of Ferrybridge

Setting out from York on 26th March with orders to gather intelligence, and if feasible, harry the Yorkists, Clifford proceeded south along the road through Tadcaster, Dintingdale, Barkston Ash, Sherburn-in-Elmet and Milford, to reach the limestone ridge upon which Brotherton stands. From here Clifford would have been able to see Yorkist work parties toiling to make the bridge passable under the voluble encouragement of Warwick and Fitzwalter. They settled in for a night of observation and ate cold rations, not daring to light a fire in case it was seen by the men at the bridge. Warwick and Fitzwalter seem to have been unaware of the enemy's presence, since they turned in for the night with only a light guard for protection.

*Plate 11: Croft Bridge, Darlington–on–Tees: similar in structure to the 15th century Ferrybridge, this bridge still carries traffic, a testament to medieval stonemasons.*

Dawn is the classic time for a surprise attack, and Clifford chose well. Probably preceded by a silent cut-throat attack on the Yorkist sentries, the Flower of Craven swept through the camp, making as much noise as possible to confuse and disorientate the sleeping men;

just woken and without time to don armour, their resistance would have been brief. Lord Fitzwalter, thinking it was a brawl among his men, came out of his tent only to be felled by a blow which later killed him. Warwick managed to grab a horse and, with the terrified survivors, set off at full gallop for Pontefract, pursued part of the way by the Lancastrians. Clifford and his men then reversed the repairs to the damaged bridge, using the materials – planks laid across the gaps – to fortify the northern end against the inevitable counter-attack.

Leaving a force to hold the bridge, Clifford then employed the tactic, (based on sound military logic and experience of the border reivers), of dispatching some men to hold the road from Castleford, through the marshes to Fairburn and onto Brotherton. His front, rear, flank and escape route thus secured, he took up a position – probably around the Brotherton end of the causeway, beyond bowshot from the south bank - where he could observe both his forces. From here he could react to events, reinforcing and resupplying the men at the bridge who would bear the full brunt of any Yorkist attack; and also withdraw easily, knowing that the Yorkists would soon realise that the bridge was only held by a small force, one they would have to sweep aside for their advance to continue.

Meanwhile news of Clifford's dawn attack caused panic amongst the Yorkists at Pontefract; it would take strenuous efforts by their commanders to calm the relatively inexperienced troops confronted by the bloodied survivors. Once Warwick had gasped out his message that the bridge was lost, he allegedly displayed a gift for theatricality which, we are told, helped to settle jangled nerves: he killed his horse and loudly proclaimed that he would fight shoulder to shoulder with any that would fight along with him. No doubt the sceptical amongst the troops would realise that he had other horses; any with a classical education would know that the gesture was not even original - Spartacus said and did something similar on the eve of his defeat by Roman legions in 71BC.

The next hours were hectic. Orders were swiftly given to prepare to advance to Ferrybridge, three miles away; the camp was struck, tents and stores quickly packed, armour put on, weapons and arrows issued, and the troops organised into marching order. Reaching Ferrybridge at about midday, the Yorkists moved into the attack by throwing in an infantry assault along the ruined bridge. Clifford had made his dispositions well; behind cover they could shoot at point-blank range into the massed ranks of troops waiting to get on to the bridge, (at best only 15 feet wide, the width useable to troops now reduced to that of a spandrel wall about 1 or 2 feet wide; a spandrel is the longitudinal stiffening wall of a bridge on top of the arch across which the roadway is laid). At a range of 45 yards or less the clothyard shaft shot from a warbow is murderously effective, achieving deep penetration even through plate armour; for any that succeeded in reaching the Lancastrian line, there were the spearmen ready with their 10-foot long weapons. The first assault having failed, archers were brought forward to keep the defenders' heads down, and the engineers told to find a solution.

As the afternoon drew on, more assaults were thrown against the bridge's defenders, with the same result. Many of the attacking troops fell into the river to perish in the icy floodwaters, be it from their wounds, drowning, or the heart-stopping shock of icy water. Attempts were made by the engineers to bridge the gaps and make rafts to take troops across the river; all failed. More men died.

Exasperated at the singular lack of success, and conscious of the need to restart the stalled advance, the high command ordered Lord Fauconberg to take his mounted troops and, following the road to Castleford, then the Fairburn road along the north bank of the river, counter-move via Brotherton to drive off or kill the defenders to take and secure the bridgehead. This he proceeded to do.

Intent on hanging on to the bridge until the last possible moment, Clifford's men had beaten off several attacks and inflicted stinging losses on Edwards's troops – up to 3000 casualties, according to Jean de Waurin, a contemporary chronicler. Probably taking advantage of the gathering dusk, the Flower of Craven slipped away to rejoin firstly their comrades at the end of the causeway, then move on to Brotherton. This they achieved just in time; the lead troops of Fauconberg's flanking attack ran into the previously planned ambush and took casualties, while the Flower of Craven departed along the Great North Road to, as they thought, the safety of their own lines.

As the action at Ferrybridge unfolded, other troops on both sides were busy. Having successfully crossed at Castleford, the Yorkist reconnaissance along and in the area of the Roman road ensured that an alternative route was available for the heavy cavalry and supply train to advance over the Aire. Safe passage for the supply train was vital, given that even a slimmed down convoy could be several miles long and, travelling at c. 12 miles per day, a slow and sitting target; an attack on, or loss of these supplies, would badly disrupt the Yorkist advance. Light cavalry may therefore have moved into the area between the Tadcaster Road and the Roman Ridge Road to act as a forward screen to protect the supply train, a tripwire in the event of a Lancastrian sally south, and to interdict both the Roman road and the Great North Road. Alternatively they may have taken Fauconberg's route via Fairburn to Brotherton, then followed the army north along the Tadcaster road.

Meanwhile, by 28th March, Somerset and the Lancastrian army had moved into their previously reconnoitred positions at Towton; Clifford's stubborn defence at Ferrybridge had given him a vital 24 hours to plan and dispose, and for his troops to rest and make last minute adjustments for the now inevitable clash of arms…

**The Battle of Dintingdale**

The success of Fauconberg's pincer move was vital to Yorkist plans. It has been surmised that his aim was to capture and kill Clifford, but this belies the true purpose of the flanking move; the death of Clifford and his men would be a bonus, but the prime focus was not revenge – it was *to secure the bridgehead.* Thus Fauconberg swung south from Brotherton after the skirmish with the Flower of Craven as they withdrew down the causeway, and finally retook the north end of the bridge. This enabled Edward to make repairs enough to move his infantry across and form up on the north side; man-packing only vital military stores they started their advance in their divisions.

Following the successful disengagement from Ferrybridge, Clifford and John, Lord Neville, gathered their remaining forces and led them north to rejoin the main army at Towton, proceeding via the Tadcaster Road through Milford and Sherburn-in-Elmet. The horses would have been tired, having been pushed by their riders' need to avoid pursuit by Fauconberg's men; the men would also have been tired, and some probably wounded, after their hours of combat, and doubtless looking forward to a well-earned rest after their efforts.

But what happened next is stark fact. The Flower of Craven were ambushed at Dintingdale and wiped out, with Clifford himself – after receiving a fatal arrow wound to the throat - decapitated and, according to Clifford family tradition, 'tumbled headless into a pit of promiscuous bodies' (see Fig. 5).

There is some debate over why this senior and trusted commander was ambushed and destroyed so close to his own army. It has been suggested that Somerset did not support him due to some personality clash and enmity; was Clifford 'hung out to dry' by a superior officer jealous of a too-popular and effective subordinate, who saw this as an opportunity to rid himself of an irritant? This is possible; there are however more feasible alternatives. It is generally accepted that Somerset formed the Lancastrian line across where Dacre's Cross now stands. This is on the reverse slope from Dintingdale and as such is out of direct sight of the road and ambush site; equally importantly it is out of earshot. On this basis Somerset would not have been able to see, (especially in the gathering gloom of a March evening), or hear either Clifford's approach or the fight, so would have been unaware of the need to take action to support him.

Was Clifford's demise due to organisational faults and/or time pressures? Somerset and his officers would have been ocupied with plans for what they all knew would be a decisive encounter; did they simply omit to make arrangements for returning scouts? Did they omit to delegate authority to subordinates so that they had the leeway to make decisions as the situation demanded without having to refer the matter upwards through the chain of command? If so, the action at Dintingdale could have been over and done with, and the Flower of Craven wiped out, before a reaction could be made. On this basis, it is a matter of too little, too late.

Possibly arrangements had been made with this eventuality in mind; as such there may have been a small force based around Dintingdale to act both as a forward screen and to meet Clifford and guide him in. But if this group had been destroyed by the Yorkists as mentioned above, it would have left Clifford, expecting a friendly force, open to attack when he was least expecting it. He may even have advanced ahead of his men, removing his face armour in order to recognise and be recognised. Struck down in the first volley, he would have been unable to rally his men, who followed him quickly to their deaths.

*Plate.12: Dintingdale: the junction of the A162 and road to Saxton (Headwell Lane), just north of Barkston Ash. This area is popularly believed to be where John Clifford, John Neville and the Flower of Craven ran into a Yorkist interdiction force and met their end.*

44

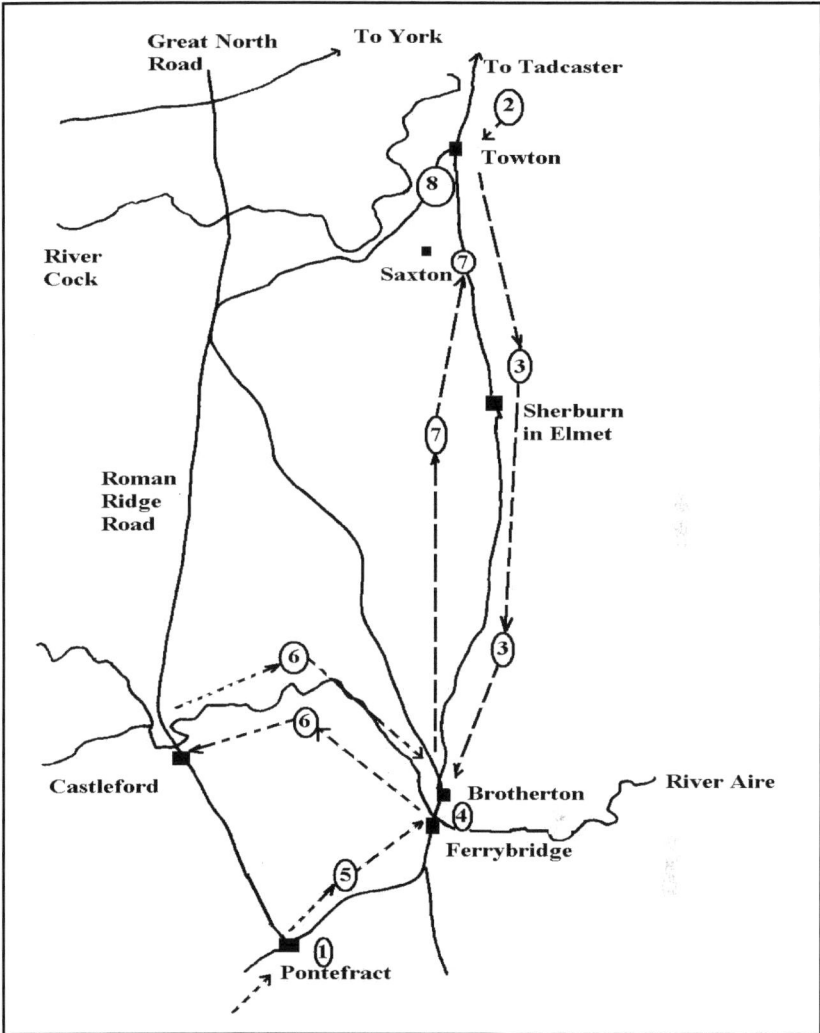

*Figure 5: Key events at Ferrybridge/Dintingdale. 1 – Pontefract Castle & Ferrybridge crossing secured by Yorkists (27th March). 2 – 3 – Somerset heads for Towton, Clifford for Ferrybridge. 4 – Clifford's dawn attack (March 28th). 5 – Yorkist counter-attack. 6 – Fauconberg's flanking attack via Castleford; 7 – Clifford withdraws and is killed at Dintingdale before 8 – the Battle of Towton.*

**Information for Visitors to Ferrybridge and Dintingdale:**

Although the 1797 bridge is no longer open to motor traffic, it forms the start line for exploring the battle site on foot; parking is available by the old Toll House, situated between the two bridges.

From the eastern parapet (right hand side) of the 1797 bridge, both the width of the river and the probable line of the 1300s bridge, (approximately the line of the modern steel bridge), can be seen. This is where the massively superior Yorkist force was held up for hours by Clifford's Flower of Craven, with the chantry chapel on its north side turned into a strongpoint. Cross to the other parapet to see the village of Brotherton; the main road gives the approximate line of the stone-built causeway along which Clifford withdrew and the Yorkists advanced to Towton.

A footpath leading down to a grassy meadow can be followed to Brotherton and its church of Edward the Confessor, where Lord Fitzwalter was reputedly buried after dying from the wound sustained in Clifford's dawn attack on Ferrybridge. From here the route of the action can be walked, although be aware that the 9 miles/ 14.4 km from Ferrybridge to Barkston Ash follows the A162, a busy road with little in the way of footpaths for much of its length.

For those going by car, take the turn off for Brotherton and the A162; you are now on the road used by Clifford and the Yorkist army. Look left going through Burton Salmon ; over the open high ground – ideal cavalry country - lies the Roman Ridge Road, part of the Great North Road. After 3 miles/4.8 km you will come to the junction of the A63 and the A162, the approximate limit of a horse at the gallop; from here Clifford's horses would have been walked in order to rest them.

Further on lie South Milford and Sherburn-in-Elmet; the A162 bypasses these settlements but you can turn off and follow the old road through their centres. For those seeking refreshment there are several hostelries including The Black Bull public house and The Swan hotel in South Milford; also here is Steeton Hall, a fine manorial gatehouse dating from the 14th century and worth a visit.

Continue through South Milford to Sherburn-in-Elmet; if you wish to view the fine Gothic Church of All Saints, turn left at the traffic lights onto the B1222 (Church Hill), follow it up the hill and you will see All Saints on the right. Towton plateau, scene of carnage on Palm Sunday 1461, is visible from the north wall of the churchyard.

*Plate 13: All Saints Church, Sherburn-in-Elmet; from the tower Yorkist commanders could survey the route up to Saxton and Towton, and the plateau where battle would be joined.*

Resuming your drive north up the A162 towards Tadcaster and York, you will pass through Barkston Ash and another fine pub, The Ash Tree. A little further on lies Dintingdale and the left turn (Headwell Lane) to Saxton, where Clifford met his end (see Plate 12). It was close to here that 19th century workmen, quarrying stone for road improvments, found a number of skeletons, one of which was headless. Could this have been the unfortunate Lord Clifford?

**Directions to Ferrybridge:**

Ferrybridge is easily accessible by car; turn off the M62 at junction 33 and follow the signs for Ferrybridge. Take the 2$^{nd}$ turning onto the B6136, and as you round the bend in the road you will see the 1797 bridge in front of you.

**Other Local Sites of Interest:**

**Ferrybridge Henge**

This Neolithic henge monument is c. 590 feet in diameter, with two ditches and a bank; finds including a 2400-year-old chariot burial have been unearthed here. Ferrybridge is the furthest south of Yorkshire's henges, and the only one in West Yorkshire. The site is of national importance and is protected from unauthorised change as a scheduled ancient monument; despite this it is under threat from ploughing.

Situated in farmland between the A1(M), M62, and Ferrybridge power station, there is unfortunately little to see, and no public access to the site. The grid reference is SE47462424, (OS Explorer sheet 289), where it is marked simply as 'henge'; as you head from Castleford towards Ferrybridge on the B6136 with the power station on your left, the henge lies opposite in fields on the right.

Further information on Ferrybridge Henge can be found on the websites http://en.wikipedia.org/wiki/Ferrybridge_Henge and http://www.knottingley.org/history/ferryhenge/fbridgehenge.

**St Andrew's Church, Pontefract Road, Ferrybridge, WF11 8PN**

This charming little church dates from Norman times and has a number of interesting architectural features. Originally situated about a mile away near the River Aire in an area notorious for flooding, it was dismantled stone by stone, transported to its current site, and rebuilt in the 1950s.

To visit St Andrew's, take Junction 33 from the M62, then the first exit off the roundabout signed for A162 Ferrybridge. Continue up the Ferrybridge bypass, passing the turnoff marked A645 Pontefract. Take the next left marked B6136 Ferrybridge, and follow the curve of the road to the T-junction (opposite you will see the old Toll House and 1789 bridge).

Turn left at the bottom of the slip road, and, heading towards Castleford, go under the railway bridge. Then take the first left onto Castleford Lane, continue to the T-junction with Pontefract Road, and you will see the church on the other side of the road. Roadside parking is available.

The original site of St Andrew's Church can also still be seen at Fryston, grid reference SE478248 (OS Explorer Sheet 289), but is now largely overgrown and not signposted, nor is it detailed on the map. The location is described in an 1871 publication by C. Forest, 'The History of Knottingley in the Parish of Pontefract', as being:

*'...approached from Ferrybridge through an avenue of fine old willows, gradually disclosing the view as the visitor advances. Its situation is most lonely and secluded; closed in by the wooded grounds of Fryston Hall behind, and from the view in front by the high rampart of the North Eastern Railway, which runs close to its hallowed precinths. There is an air of solemn stillness about the venerable pile, well suited for 'lonely contemplation', but rudely broken by the scream and rattle of the train as it rushes past.'*

# PART 4: TOWTON

## The Crooked Billet /St Mary's Chapel, Lead

The Lancastrians' objective was now to prevent the Yorkists from seizing the northern capital of York, where the royal family were ensconced; and in the process, to defeat Edward's army and extinguish his challenge to the crown.

By delaying the Yorkist advance at Ferrybridge, Lord Clifford had bought his comrades valuable time to deploy for battle on ground of their choosing. The most obvious, and apparently advantageous, place lay beside the Tadcaster road nine miles south of York: the northern slope of Towton Vale, the highest piece of land between York and Ferrybridge. Accordingly, by the evening of 28th March 1461, the Lancastrians had encamped around the village of Towton to await the arrival of their opponents. John Cliford's death notwithstanding, the Dukes of Exeter and Somerset, the Earls of Northumberland, Devon and Wiltshire, the Lords Dacre, Hungerford and Rivers and their companions were no doubt in good heart; their large army was well fed and rested, buoyed up by recent victories at Wakefield and St Albans, and probably confident (or over-confident) that they would prevail through sheer weight of numbers.

The Yorkists, on the other hand, had just made a long forced march up from London, and sustained casualties they had perhaps not foreseen during Lord Clifford's spirited defence of Ferrybridge. Now they had to camp in bitter weather around the villages of Lead and Saxton, south of Towton Vale; the 15th century chronicler Jean de Waurin wrote, 'it was so cold with snow and ice that it was pitiful to see men and horses suffer, especially as they were badly fed'.

Tradition has it that King Edward camped on the site of The Crooked Billet public house – possibly even at an inn of that name attached to the now vanished hamlet of Lead. (Its odd name may be derived from a crooked billet, or bent piece of wood, being hung outside the building to advertise its function, an early form of pub sign).

*Plate 14 : The present-day Crooked Billet*

Some of Edward's men may have sought shelter in Lead itself. The name 'Lead' is derived from the Anglo-Saxon *hleodu* or wooded enclosure, and a small farming community had existed there since before the Norman Conquest. Lead is described in *Domesday Book* as having two acres of meadow, two caracates of taxable land (a caracate being the amount of land a team of eight oxen could plough in a year), three villagers and two smallholders (presumably together with their families, who are not listed).

Its chapel, St Mary's, was probably built as the family chapel of the Tyas family; the grave slabs of Baldwin Tyas, his wife Marjorie and their son Franco can be seen by the altar. Originally it was a larger building, having a chancel as well as a nave, the location of which is marked by the railed enclosure abutting the east end. Then in 1392 the manor of Lead was inherited by Thomas Scargill, possibly via his wife Joan (or Johanna) Tyas; and by 1461, Lead's inhabitants were working for the Scargills, whose timbered manor house may have stood on the site of nearby Lead Hall Farm. Some people believe that

Lead was destroyed in the Battle of Towton - but this seems unlikely as it still existed in the 16th century, mentioned as a 'hamlet' in the *Itinerary* of John Leland. So it seems reasonable to assume that some Yorkist troops spent Palm Sunday eve here – perhaps within the peaceful walls of St Mary's, praying for their deliverance on the morrow.

*Plate 15: St Mary's Chapel, Lead*

**Information for Visitors to The Crooked Billet/St Mary's:**

**The Crooked Billet, Wakefield Road, Saxton, Tadcaster, North Yorkshire LS24 9QN; telephone 01937 557389**

The Crooked Billet is open year-round, serving meals, snacks, alcohol and beverages. A Portacabin in the car-park contains displays and information from Towton Battlefield Society and the Churches Conservation Trust (free admission, key available from the bar); and on the third Sunday of the month, members of the Battlefield Society hold a longbow archery session in the field adjoining the car-park. The two apple trees in this field are historically and horticulturally significant. Both are old and now very rare varieties, survivors from the inn's 19th century kitchen garden: on the side nearest the road, a Transparente de Croncels, and opposite, a Yorkshire Greening. Both varieties were popular in the Victorian period, the Yorkshire Greening often being used to make a tangy sauce to accompany roast goose (as indicated by its alternative name, Yorkshire Goose-Sauce).

## St Mary's, Lead

In the field opposite The Crooked Billet you can see all that remains of Lead village: a series of grass-covered humps and depressions representing dwellings, ponds, an enclosure, a dovecot and a hollow-way, surrounding the now isolated and reduced chapel of St Mary's.

St Mary's is managed by the Churches Conservation Trust, assisted by the Friends of Lead; it is open year-round and admission is free, although donations to help with its upkeep are appreciated. It is no longer a place of regular worship, although an annual service is held on Rogation Sunday, the 6th Sunday of Easter, together with special events including open days, and a Christmas carol service.

The chapel can be reached by a rough grass-covered track from the field gate opposite The Crooked Billet - beware fast-moving traffic when crossing the B1217. Although the track can be crossed by wheelchair, (pusher recommended), the gate of the fenced security enclosure around the south door does not open widely enough to allow wheelchair or pushchair access to the interior. This is a simple space containing a Norman font, the 13th century Tyas grave slabs, and an 18th century rustic pulpit, clerk's pew, reading desk and painted texts; the east window behind the altar was reglazed in 1982, and incorporates a stained and painted glass panel depicting the white boar of King Richard III, donated by the Yorkshire Branch of the Richard III Society.

Further information about St Mary's can be found on the Churches Conservation Trust website www.visitchurches.org.uk.

**Directions to The Crooked Billet/St Mary's**

**From the M1:** Leave the motorway at the Garforth exit, (Junction 47), and turn left from the slip-road (B1217), following the brown signs for Lotherton Hall. Remain on the B1217, and soon after passing Lotherton Hall you will come to The Crooked Billet ahead on the right, and St Mary's on the left.

**All Saint's Church and Towton Monument, Main Street, Saxton**

On Palm Sunday eve, other Yorkist troops may have sought shelter from the biting weather in the larger village of Saxton, which merits a visit to see another site associated with Towton: the church of All Saints.

All Saints was built in the late 12th century on the site of an earlier Anglo-Saxon church, of which nothing remains but a decorated cross head displayed in the north sanctuary. Its churchyard contains the remains of a number of victims from the battle. Some, formerly buried in two mass graves on the battlefield, were reinterred there in 1484 by order of Richard III; it is also the final resting place of skeletons unearthed during building works at Towton Hall in 1990. However, the most prominent victim to lie in Saxton is Ranulph, Lord Dacre, who was famously buried with his horse. Dacre's tomb can be seen in the churchyard near the north-east corner of the building (Plate 16). It is made of Craven limestone surrounded by iron rails, and the inscription reads: 'Here lies Randolph Lord of Dacre and Gilsland; a true knight valiant in battle in the service of King Henry VI, who died on Palm Sunday 29 March 1461 on whose soul may God have mercy, Amen'.

Beside Dacre's tomb you will see the monument erected in 2005 by Towton Battlefield Society to mark the re-interment of remains from Towton Hall, and to commemorate all who fell in the battle. Created by local sculptor and Society member Steven Hines, the monument is designed to evoke Towton in every aspect, from its arrowhead form to the subtle topographic image of the battlefield worked into its inscription.

*Plate 16: Dacre's tomb and Towton monument in All Saints churchyard, Saxton*

**Directions to All Saints from The Crooked Billet:**

**On foot:** The church can be reached by a public footpath across farmland from The Crooked Billet, a distance of c. 1 mile/1.6 km.

Climb the rough steps at the right-hand corner of the car-park (with your back to the pub), and follow the path beside the hedge to a second set of steps. This leads you to a trodden path striking diagonally to the right across a large arable field. After crossing this field, turn left at the track then right at the hedgerow to dog-leg around the field beyond. Look out for the arrow sign and stone stile in the hedge on the right; cross here to go through the grounds of a private house and emerge onto Main Street in Saxton. Turn left onto Main Street for the historic Greyhound public house; All Saints lies just beyond on the corner of Main Street and Dam Lane. With two sets of steps and a stile to cross, this route is inaccessible for wheelchair users, and unsuitable for people with walking difficulties. Nor is it a particularly interesting walk, its main virtue being that it is the shortest, most direct route between The Crooked Billet and Saxton. As the route passes through a working farm and private gardens, dogs must be kept on a lead.

**By car:** Turn right from The Crooked Billet car-park in the direction of Towton, and take the first right (signposted for Saxton) from the B1217 onto Dam Lane. Follow Dam Lane to the T-junction with Main Street and you will see All Saints on the right.

**The Battle of Towton**

On the morning of Palm Sunday, March 29$^{th}$ 1461, the two armies broke camp and marched to the field, most probably using the track between Saxton and Towton corresponding to the present B1217. Given the treacherous conditions, it is interesting to speculate how many casualties – slips, sprains and broken wrists or ankles – the troops sustained even as they deployed on the icy hillsides; although at this stage, neither side can have realised the full cataclysmic impact the lie of the land and the weather were about to play in the course of events.

Like Mortimer's Cross, the battlefield area at Towton is roughly triangular, defined by roads and a river: to the east and north/north-west, the road from Ferrybridge via Towton to Tadcaster (the present A162); to the south, the lane between Saxton and Dintingdale; and to the west, the meandering River Cock (often known as Cock Beck). However, unlike Mortimer's Cross, the land enclosed by these features is a high exposed plateau, bisected almost centrally by Towton Vale. The precipitous drop on the western edge overlooking the Cock must initially have been viewed as an advantage by the Lancastrians, since it anchored and protected their right flank as they deployed on the northern ridge of Towton Vale. Facing them on the lower southern slope were the Yorkists, with their left flank anchored by the steep hill down into the field now known as Bloody Meadow.

Concentrations of arrowheads found on the field indicate that hostilities at Towton began in customary style with an archery exchange, in which the Yorkists gained an early advantage. Unusually, the wind was blowing from the south, driving snow into the Lancastrians' faces. Observing this, Edward's canny commander Lord Fauconberg instructed his archers to advance thirty paces, shoot a volley and retire. As arrows fell into their ranks, the Lancastrian archers shot back; but blinded by snow, were unable to see their arrows, shot against the wind, falling harmlessly short. Many of these were subsequently retrieved by the Yorkist archers, thus enabling them to shoot a double barrage with devastating effect; and as the Lancastrians took heavy casualties, they had no choice but to leave the favourable higher ground and advance for the melee.

Hours of fierce hand-to-hand fighting ensued on ground littered with spent arrows and corpses; and we know that the weapons used included some artillery, thanks to recent discoveries of a piece of iron-cored lead shot and two fragments from hand-guns which had exploded in use – the earliest conclusive proof of gunnery on a Wars of the Roses battlefield. At some point during the fighting, Lord Dacre, who had retired from the front line for refreshment, shared the same fate as Lord Clifford – according to tradition, an archer concealed in a burr tree shot him in the throat when he lowered his bevor to drink.

As the day progressed, notwithstanding the advantage the Yorkists had gained in the opening barrage, weight of Lancastrian numbers began to prevail. If the Yorkists had been pushed back over the southern edge of the plateau towards Saxton, the outcome would have been very different; as it was, they were saved in the nick of time by the Duke of Norfolk. Norfolk is thought to have been delayed at Pontefract, possibly by illness; but now, as his fresh troops arrived from Ferrybridge and smashed into the Lancastrian left flank, the tide of battle turned decisively in the Yorkists' favour. The battle lined skewed as the Lancastrians, already tired and now demoralised by the appearance of reinforcements, started to fall back – with the effect that their right flank was forced off the steep western edge of the plateau.

Once this downward trajectory had begun, there was no stopping it – fighting back up the slope would have been hard enough in summer weather; on the conditions of this Palm Sunday, it was impossible. Desperate troops skidded down the steep icy hillsides, many being killed by pursuing Yorkists in Bloody Meadow. Others plunged into Cock Beck, hoping to ford it and escape – and here again, the weather played a fatal part. Swollen by recent precipitation, the river was in spate; men could have perished from shock and exposure in the freezing waters, or been dragged down by the weight of soaked garments; and their plight was compounded by their over-confident commanders having broken down the bridges to prevent them being used as a line of retreat by routing Yorkists. Now the slain piled up as grisly 'bridges of bodies' across the river; and according to tradition, the carnage was so great that the Cock ran red with blood all the way to its confluence with the River Wharfe.

This catastrophic rout, the worst of the Wars of the Roses, soon infected the whole Lancastrian army and troops fled in every direction, pursued in some cases as far as Tadcaster. There are also traditions of fighting having occurred nearby at Sherburn-in-Elmet and Kirkby Wharfe, and archaeology has shown that some action took place in or near Towton itself: the famous mass graves excavated in and around Towton Hall in 1996. The skeletons show evidence of the most brutal savagery: multiple arrow and blade strikes, including many wounds to the head and face (suggesting that the victims were not wearing helmets). Possibly some of these soldiers had been wounded earlier in the fighting, and withdrawn to the Lancastrian camp for treatment; alternatively, they may have been hunted down in the rout, and despatched with what can only be described as 'overkill'. Either way, it is likely that they were buried in a convenient piece of hallowed ground: the environs of the lost chapel of St Mary at Towton, which has probably been subsumed within the footprint of the present Towton Hall.

The size of the armies that fought at Towton, and the casualty figures, are hotly disputed. Contemporary sources speak of 20,000 to 38,000 killed, in which case we might estimate the day began with

50,000 or more troops on the field. But whatever the true figures, Towton certainly embroiled a large number of senior magnates and their men from all over the British Isles, as well as (in all probability) mercenaries from Burgundy and France; and whether it really was, as is sometimes claimed, 'the biggest and bloodiest battle ever fought on British soil', it does seem to have been noted at the time as a particularly terrible conflict. Among the Lancastrian dead were Henry Percy, Earl of Northumberland, John, Lord Neville, and the veteran commander Andrew Trollope, engineers of the Duke of York's calamity at Wakefield three months previously – and so, by the end of Palm Sunday 1461, the day had been resoundingly won by the Yorkists, consolidating Edward IV's claim on the crown.

**Towton Battlefield Trail**

Thanks to a partnership between the land-owners, Leeds Royal Armouries, Rural England and Towton Battlefield Society, visitors to Towton can now enjoy a self-directed tour around the battlefield on a new footpath (2 miles/3.2 km long), complete with interpretation boards at key vantage points (see Fig. 6 and Plates 18 and 20).

**Short Tour: Dacre's Cross**

If you are pressed for time or unable to walk long distances you can take a mini-tour, with the best overviews of the heart of the battlefield, from the monument beside the B1217 between Saxton and Towton popularly known as Dacre's Cross (Plate 17).

Despite its name, the monument has no known connection with Lord Dacre – although it does have an interesting and chequered history. As it stands today, Dacre's Cross comprises three elements – a wheel-headed cross, a tapering shaft and a socket, set on a modern plinth. The original shaft, locally called 'Dacre's Stone', was described in 1904 as leaning, half-buried, carved near the top on two sides with large, deeply engraved crosses, and minus the head (which in 1882 was recorded as lying beneath a holly bush in the hedgerow). Like the head and socket, this shaft is believed to have come from the lost chapel at Towton, and the monument may have originally stood as a wayside cross, boundary marker or battle memorial. (Sadly, the whereabouts of the original shaft are now unknown). By 1929, the head had been retrieved and wedged directly into the socket, until a Mr. James Ogden provided a new shaft and plinth, creating the monument in the form we see today.

*Plate 17 : Dacre's Cross*

Starting opposite the monument, a stretch of new footpath 0.3 miles/ 0.5 km long (towards Saxton) takes you to the first battlefield interpretation board, 'The Battle Lines', showing how the armies were deployed on the field. At the cross itself, Board 2 gives an aerial view of the whole Battlefield Trail, while Board 3 introduces the 'Kings in Conflict', Henry VI and Edward IV. A short stretch of rough track (wheelchair accessible, pusher recommended) then leads from Dacre's Cross to Board 4, 'The Battle Reaches its Climax' and Board 5, 'Battlefield Archaeology'. These boards overlook the steep drop into 'Bloody Meadow', and it is easy to imagine Yorkist archers picking off the Lancastrians as they routed towards Cock Beck. (Also note landscape traces of earlier, more peaceful activities: the strip lynchets on the hillside to your left, evidence of Iron Age farming).

*Plate 18: Interpretation boards 2 & 3 at Bloody Meadow*

**Full Tour: Bloody Meadow to Towton**

More energetic walkers can continue the Trail from this point, circling the western edge of Towton plateau past Boards 6 – 8:

'Weapons of the Wars of the Roses', 'The Rout of the Lancastrians', and 'Armour of the Wars of the Roses'. The rises and undulations in the ground on your right make it impossible to see the full battlefield from this perspective – just as it would have been impossible for the fleeing Lancastrians to see the vertiginous drop for which they were heading (on your left) until it was too late.

Just past Board 9, 'The Bridge of Bodies', you will come to a brown metal gate and a fork in the track, the footpath to Stutton, where you can take an interesting digression from the main Battlefield Trail. If you follow this path, (which is narrow, rough, steep in places and not recommended for people with walking difficulties), to the left down the hill, you will come to a modern wooden bridge across Cock Beck - believed to mark one of the sites where bodies piled high in the water. (Beware the vicious horse-flies in hot weather!).

*Plate 19 : The 'Bridge of Bodies'*

Otherwise, remaining on the Trail takes you to Old London Road, the probable route used by the Lancastrians in marching from York. The tenth and final interpretation board, 'The Village', is situated here, showing an aerial view of Towton with its medieval ridge-and-furrow fields, and Towton Hall, site of the Lancastrian camp and St Mary's Chapel, where the famous mass graves were found.

*Plate 20 : Board 10 on the Old London Road into Towton*

(Approaching Towton Hall, you will pass a field on the right where a battle commemoration is held every Palm Sunday by Towton Battlefield Society and its affiliated re-enactment group, The Frei Compagnie. The event features a living history camp, memorial service, archery and sword and combat demonstrations on the field, traders and exhibitors in the modern barn by the field gate, and a programme of guided battlefield walks in the morning).

When you reach the bottom of Old London Road, turn right at the Rockingham Arms, right again at the junction with the B1217, and you will shortly pick up the footpath on the right to return to your starting point at Dacre's Cross.

To Stutton

Bridge of
Bodies

9

To Tadcaster/
York

10

8

Old London
Road

N

Rockingham Arms

TOWTON

7

6

B1217

Renshaw
Wood

4 & 5

LANCASTRIAN
ARMY

A162

Dacre's
Cross
2 & 3

River Cock

Bloody
Meadow

1

Castle Hill
Wood

YORKIST ARMY

Burr Tree
(Dacre's
Fall)

B1217

Saxton Lane

SAXTON

Dinting Dale

Norfolk's
Advance

St Mary's,
Lead

Crooked Billet

Dam Lane

All
Saints/
Dacre's Tomb/
Towton Monument

To M1/
Leeds

A162

To Ferrybridge

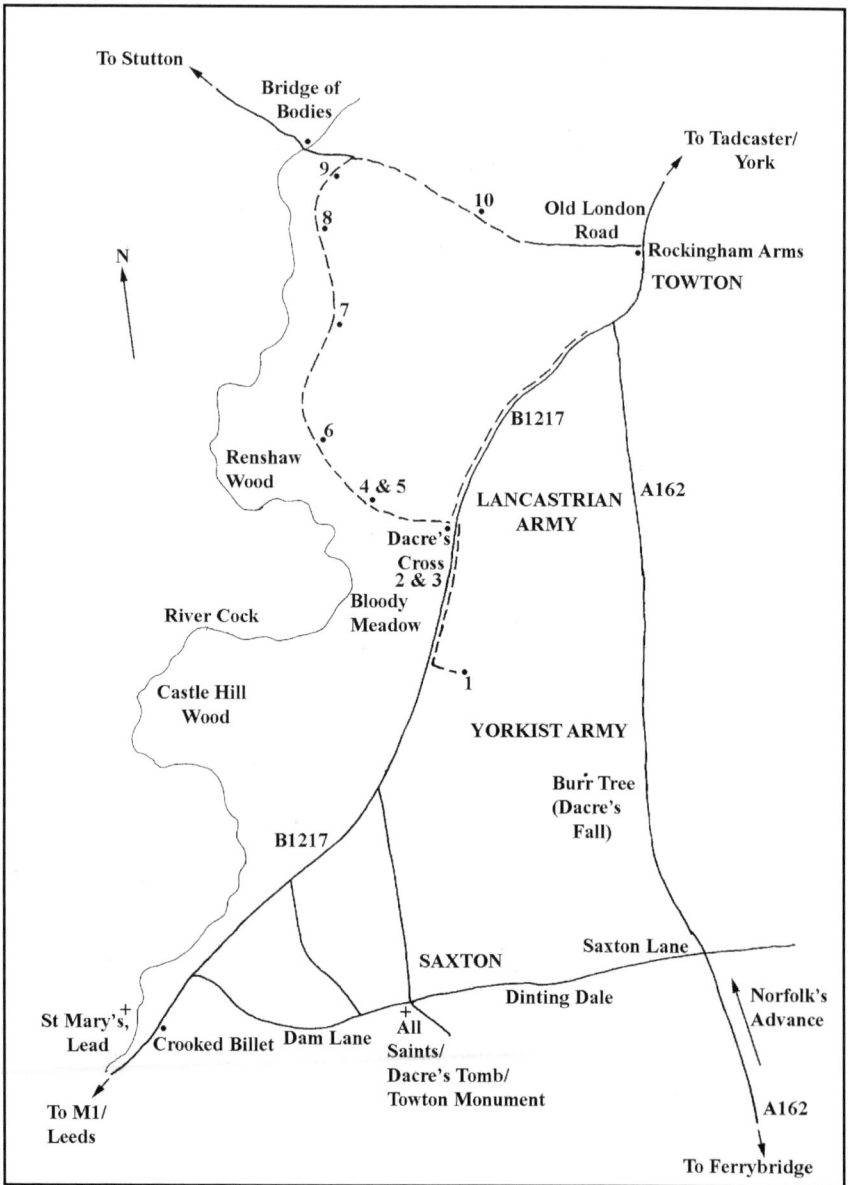

*Figure 6: Map of Towton Battlefield Trail (dotted line) showing the position of interpretation boards*

**Information for Visitors to Towton Battlefield Trail:**

Towton Battlefield Trail can be walked free of charge at any time of year. A limited amount of parking is available in a lay-by at Dacre's Cross if you wish to walk the Trail as described above. Alternatively, patrons of the Rockingham Arms may park in the pub car-park, proceed up Old London Road, and take the interpretation boards in reverse order around to Bloody Meadow and Dacre's Cross, then return down the roadside footpath to Towton - with the advantage of ending at the pub for refreshments! Or if you prefer to have a guide, Towton Battlefield Society members lead two walks a month, typically on the second and fourth Sundays, starting at 10.30am from the Rockingham Arms – check the Society's website (see below) for details, or to arrange walks, talks or group visits at other times.

But however you walk it, be aware that the Trail is rough in places, with some moderate gradients, and can become very muddy in wet weather. It is unsuitable for pushchairs and wheelchair users; stout footwear is essential, and since the plateau is high, exposed and windy, warm/waterproof clothing is also recommended. The route passes through a working farm, so visitors are requested to remain on the footpath, not to drop litter, and to keep dogs on a lead.

For further information about the Battle of Towton, the Battlefield Trail and Towton Battlefield Society, see the TBS website www.towton.org.uk; or contact the Chairman, Mark Taylor, by email on chairman@towton.org.uk or by telephone on 01302 882488.

**The Rockingham Arms, Main Street, Towton, Leeds LS24 9PB; telephone 01937 530948**

The Rockingham Arms is open year-round, serving meals, snacks, alcohol and beverages. A Towton Battlefield Society Information Centre is scheduled to open on the first floor in Spring 2012, and in the garden to the rear you will see grafts from the two apple trees from The Crooked Billet, transplanted in 2011 by the Northern Fruit Group.

**Directions to Towton Battlefield Trail:**

**From the Crooked Billet to Dacre's Cross:**

Turn right out of the Crooked Billet car-park onto the B1217. You will shortly pass the first battlefield board in fields on the right, and Dacre's Cross 0.3 miles/0.5 km further on, on the left.

**From Dacre's Cross to Towton/Rockingham Arms:**

Continue past the monument to the T-junction of the B1217 and the A162 (Main Street), and turn left. The driveway with stone columns on the left, just past the junction, is the entrance to the grounds of Towton Hall and visitor parking *for the Palm Sunday event only* (Towton Hall is a private residence whose grounds are not otherwise open to the public). A short distance further along Main Street is the Rockingham Arms; turn left onto Old London Road and left again for the pub car-park.

**From the A1 to Towton**: Take the A64 towards York, then the A162 south at Tadcaster. Follow the road straight into Towton; when you see the Rockingham Arms ahead on the right, turn right onto Old London Road and first left into the car-park. For Dacre's Cross/The Crooked Billet/St Mary's, continue past the Rockingham Arms and take the first right onto the B1217. You will shortly see Dacre's Cross on the right; continuing along the B1217 will bring you to The Crooked Billet on the left and St Mary's on the right.

# AFTERWORD

Although the victory at Towton had confirmed Edward IV as England's new king, his war was far from over. Hostilities continued in the north as Lancastrian loyalists strove to reinstate Henry VI, with battles fought at Hedgeley Moor and Hexham in 1464, and contests for possession of Northumbrian and Welsh castles which went on until the last stronghold, Harlech, was surrendered in 1468 – but that's another story!

# Bibliography

**Primary Sources:**

*Annales Rerum Anglicarum*, in *Letters and Papers Illustrative of the Wars of the English in France*, Vol. 2, Part 2, J. Stevenson (ed.), Rolls Series, 1864

*Calendar of State Papers and Manuscripts existing in the Archives and Collections of Milan*, A.B. Hinds (ed.), London, 1913; British History Online, www.british-history.ac.uk

*Calendar of State Papers and Manuscripts relating to English affairs existing in the Archives and Collections of Venice*, R Brown (ed.), Vol. 1, 1202-1509, 1864

*Crowland Chronicle Continuations 1459 – 1486*, N. Pronay and J. Cox (eds.), Richard III and Yorkist History Trust, Allan Sutton Publishing, 1986

*An English Chronicle of the Reigns of Richard II, Henry IV, Henry V and Henry VI*, J.S. Davies (ed.), Camden Society, 1856

'Chronicle of William Gregory, Skinner', in *Historical Collections of a Citizen of London in the Fifteenth Century*, J. Gairdner (ed.), Camden Society, 1876

Edward Halle, *The Union of the Two Noble Families of Lancaster and* York, 1550 edition, Scolar Press, 1970

*Ingulph's Chronicle of the Abbey of Croyland*, H.T. Riley (ed.), London, 1854

John Leland, 'Itinerary', Yorkshire extracts, *Yorkshire Archaeological Journal*, Vol. 10, 1889

Short English Chronicle, *Three Fifteenth Century Chronicles*, J. Gairdner (ed.), Camden Society, 1880

Jean de Waurin, *Recuil des Chroniques d'Engleterre*, W. and E. Hardy (eds.), 1891; http://en.wikipedia.org/wiki/Jean_de_Wavrin

**Secondary Sources:**

Boardman, A.W., *The Battle of Towton*, Alan Sutton Publishing Ltd., 1994

Burley, P., Elliot, M., and Watson, H., *The Battles of St Albans*, Pen

& Sword Battleground Series, 2007

Cox, H., *The Battle of Wakefield Revisited*, Herstory Writing/York Publishing Services, 2010

Dockray, K., *Henry VI, Margaret of Anjou and the Wars of the Roses: A Source Book*, Sutton Publishing, 2000

Fiorato, V., Boylston, A. and Knüsel, C. (eds.), *Blood Red Roses: The Archaeology of a Mass Grave from the Battle of Towton AD 1461*, 2nd edition, Oxbow Books, 2007

Forrest, C., *The History of Knottingley in the Parish of Pontefract*, Kessinger, 1871

Goodwin, G., *Fatal Colours: the Battle of Towton 1461*, Weidenfeld & Nicolson, 2011

Haigh, P.A., *The Battle of Wakefield 1460*, Sutton Publishing Ltd., 1996

Haigh, P.A., *From Wakefield to Towton*, Pen & Sword, 2002

Hodges, G., *Ludford Bridge and Mortimer's Cross*, Logaston Press, 1989

Santiuste, D., *Edward IV and the Wars of the Roses*, Pen & Sword Military, 2010

# ABOUT THE AUTHORS

Helen Cox originally qualified as an archaeologist, and spent nine years working in museums in Britain and the USA as a conservator-restorer. Between 1997 – 2005 she worked as a freelance heritage consultant, then took early retirement to pursue her interests in medieval history and creative writing. Based in Wakefield, Helen now works as a freelance writer, lecturer and Wars of the Roses interpreter. She has self-published two non-fiction books on the Battle of Wakefield; a novel entitled *Gondarlan*, the first volume of her historical fantasy saga *Lay of Angor*; and is currently working on the second volume, *Breath of Gaia*.

Born in 1957, Alan Stringer spent 14 years in the Territorial Army with the Royal Army Medical Corps attached to the Light Infantry, and its successor KOYLI Light Reconnaissance Battalion. He studied psychology at Leicester (1987) and Leeds (1988-91) universities, qualified as a lecturer at Huddersfield University in 1996, and is currently employed at a specialist college for blind students in Harrogate. He has a keen interest in history, particularly in the medieval period.

Both authors are active members of Towton Battlefield Society (TBS), and its affiliated Wars of the Roses re-enactment group, The Frei Compagnie, of which Helen is Secretary. Both are also keen longbow archers, Alan being co-ordinator of the TBS Palmsunday Archers group which meets at the Crooked Billet on the third Sunday of the month.

For further information about Towton Battlefield Society and the Frei Compagnie, see the Society website www.towton.org.uk.

For further information about Helen Cox and Herstory Publications, see Helen's website www.helencox-herstorywriting.co.uk.